# Humility

## Andrew Murray

Whitaker House

Scripture quotations are taken from the King James Version (KJV) of the Holy Bible.

*Editor's note:* This book has been edited for the modern reader. Words, expressions, and sentence structure have been updated for clarity and readability.

# HUMILITY

ISBN: 0-88368-110-2
Printed in the United States of America
© 1982 by Whitaker House

Whitaker House
30 Hunt Valley Circle
New Kensington, PA 15068
Visit our web site at: www.whitakerhouse.com

15 16 17 18 19 20 21 22 / 09 08 07 06 05 04 03 02

# CONTENTS

# PREFACE

There are three great motives that urge us to humility. It strengthens me as a man, as a sinner, and as a saint. The first motive we see in the heavenly hosts, in unfallen man, in Jesus as the Son of Man. The second motive appeals to us in our fallen state, and points out the only way through which we can return to our right place as men. In the third motive, we have the mystery of grace, which teaches us that, as we lose ourselves in the overwhelming greatness of redeeming love, humility becomes to us the consummation of everlasting blessedness and adoration.

In our ordinary Christian teaching, the second aspect of man as sinner has been too exclusively put in the foreground. Some have even gone to the extreme of saying that we must keep sinning if we are indeed to remain humble. Others have thought that the strength of self-condemnation is the secret of humility. And the

Christian life has suffered loss, because believers have not been distinctly guided to see that nothing is more natural and beautiful and blessed than to be nothing, so that God may be all. It has not been made clear that it is not sin that humbles us most, but grace. It is the soul, led through its sinfulness to be occupied with God in His wonderful glory as God, as Creator and Redeemer, that will truly take the lowest place before Him.

In these meditations I have, for more than one reason, almost exclusively directed attention to the humility that becomes us as men. It is not only because the connection between humility and sin is already abundantly set forth in all our Christian teaching, but because I believe that for the fullness of the Christian life, it is indispensable that prominence be given to the other aspect. If Jesus is indeed to be our example in His humility, we need to understand the principles in which it was rooted. We need to find the common ground on which we stand with Him, and in which our likeness to Him is to be attained. If we are indeed to be humble, not only before God but toward men—if humility is to be our joy—we must see that it is not just viewed as the mark of shame because of sin. It must also be understood apart from all sin as a covering with the very beauty and blessedness of heaven and of Jesus.

We will see that just as Jesus found His glory in taking the form of a servant, so also He said to us, "Whosoever would be greatest among you, shall be your servant"(Matthew 23:11). He simply taught us the blessed truth that there is nothing so divine and heavenly as being the servant and helper of all. The faithful servant who recognizes his position finds a real pleasure in supplying the wants of the master or his guests. When we see that humility is something infinitely deeper than contrition, and accept it as our participation in the life of Jesus, we will begin to learn that it is our true nobility. We will begin to understand that being servants of all is the highest fulfillment of our destiny, as men created in the image of God.

When I look back on my own religious experience, or on the Church of Christ in the world, I stand amazed at the thought of how little humility is sought after as the distinguishing feature of the discipleship of Jesus. In preaching and living, in the daily activities of the home and social life, in the more special fellowship with Christians, in the direction and performance of work for Christ—how much proof there is that humility is not esteemed the cardinal virtue. It is not considered the only root from which the graces can grow, and the one indispensable condition of true fellowship with Jesus. The accusation that those who claim to be seeking the higher holiness have not always done so with increased humility is a call to all earnest Christians to prove that meekness and lowliness of heart are the chief marks by which they follow the meek and humble Lamb of God.

# Chapter 1

## HUMILITY: THE GLORY OF THE CREATURE

*"The four and twenty elders shall cast their crowns before the throne, saying Thou art worthy, O Lord, to receive glory and honor and power: for Thou hast created all things, and for Thy pleasure they are and were created"* — Revelation 4:10-11.

When God created the universe, it was with the one object of making man the partaker of His perfection and blessedness, and of showing in it the glory of His love, His wisdom, and His power. God wished to reveal Himself in and through created beings by communicating to them as much of His own goodness and glory as they were capable of receiving. But this did not mean that man was given something which he could possess in itself, or a certain life or goodness of which he had the charge and disposal. By no means.

As God is the ever-living, ever-present, everacting One—who upholds all things by the Word of His power, and in whom all things exist—the relationship of man to God could only be one of unceasing, absolute, universal dependence. As truly as God by His power once created, so truly by that same power must God, every moment, maintain. Man need only look back to the origin of existence and he will acknowledge that he owes everything to God. Man's chief care, his highest virtue, and his only happiness, now and through all eternity, is to present himself as an empty vessel in which God can dwell and manifest His power and goodness.

The life God bestows is imparted not once and for all, but each moment continuously, by the unceasing operation of His mighty power. Humility, the place of entire dependence on God, is, from the very nature of things, the first duty and the highest virtue of man. It is the root of every virtue.

And so pride, or the loss of this humility, is the root of every sin and evil. It was when the now fallen angels began to look upon themselves with self-satisfaction that they were led to disobedience and were cast down from the light of heaven into outer darkness. When the serpent breathed the poison of his pride—the desire to be like God—into the hearts of our first parents, they, too, fell from their high estate into all the wretchedness in which man is now sunk. In all heaven and earth, pride and self-exaltation are the gate and the curse of hell. (See Note A.)

Hence, it follows that nothing can redeem us but the restoration of our lost humility, the original and only true relationship of man to God. And so Jesus came to bring humility back to earth, to make us partakers of it, and by it to save us. In heaven, He humbled Himself to become man. The humility we see in Him, He possessed in heaven; it brought Him, and He brought it, from there. Here on earth "He humbled Himself, and became obedient unto death" (Philippians 2:8). His humility gave His death its value, and so became our redemption. And now the salvation He imparts is nothing less than a communication of His own life and death, His own disposition and spirit. His own humility has become the ground and root of His relationship to God and His redeeming work. Jesus Christ took the place and fulfilled the destiny of man by His life of perfect humility. His humility is our salvation. His salvation is our humility.

And so the life of the saved ones, of the saints, must bear this stamp of deliverance from sin and full restoration to their original state. Their whole relationship to both God and man must be marked by an all-pervading humility. Without this there can be no true abiding in God's presence or experience of His favor and the power of His Spirit. Without this there can be no abiding faith or love or joy or strength. Humility is the only soil in which the graces root; the lack of humility is the sufficient explanation of every defect and failure. Humility is not so much a grace or virtue along with others; it is the root of all, because it alone assumes the right attitude before God and allows Him as God to do all. God gave us a sense of reason. Because of this, the truer our insight into the real nature or the absolute need of a command, the more ready and full our obedience to it will be. The call to humility has been too little regarded in the Church because its true nature and importance have been too little understood. It is not something which we bring to God or He bestows. It is simply *the sense of entire nothingness, which comes when we see how truly God is all, and in which we make way for God to be all.* Man must realize that this is the true nobility. He must consent to be, with his will, his mind, and his affections, the form and the vessel in which the life and glory of God are to work and manifest themselves. Then he will see that humility is simply acknowledging the truth of his position as man and yielding to God His place.

In the life of earnest Christians, of those who pursue and profess holiness, humility ought to be the chief mark of their uprightness. It is often said that it is not so. One reason may be that in the teaching and example of the Church, humility has never had that place of supreme importance which rightfully belongs to it. This results from the neglect of this truth: that although sin is a powerful motive to humility, there is one of still wider and mightier influence—that which makes the angels, that which made Jesus, that which makes the holiest of saints in heaven, so humble. That is, that the first and chief mark of the relationship of man with God, the secret of his biessedness, is the humility and nothingness which leaves God free to be all.

I am sure there are many Christians who will confess that their experience has been very much like my own in this—that we had long known the Lord without realizing that meekness and lowliness of heart should be the distinguishing feature of the disciple, as they were of the Master. Such humility is not a thing that will come on its own. It must be made the object of special desire, prayer, faith, and practice. As we study the Word, we will see what very distinct and often repeated instructions Jesus gave His disciples on this point, and how slow they were in understanding Him.

Let us, from the beginning, admit that there is nothing so natural to man, nothing so insidious and hidden from our sight, nothing so difficult and dangerous, as pride. Let us feel that nothing but a very determined and persevering waiting on God and Christ will disclose how lacking we are in the grace of humility, and how weak we are to obtain what we seek. Let us study the character of Christ until our souls are filled with the love and admiration of His humility. And let us believe that, when we are broken down under a sense of our pride, and realize our inability to cast it out, Jesus Christ Himself will give us this grace as a part of His wondrous life within us.

## Chapter 2

## HUMILITY: THE SECRET
## OF REDEMPTION

*"Let this mind be in you, which was also in
Christ Jesus: Who . . . made Himself of no reputation, and took upon Him the form of a servant, . . . He humbled Himself, and became
obedient unto death, even the death of the cross.
Wherefore God also hath highly exalted
Him"*—Philippians 2:5, 7-9.

No tree can grow except on the root from
which it sprang. Through all its existence it can
only live with the life that was in the seed that
gave it being. This truth, in its application to the
first and the Second Adam, can greatly help us
to understand both the need and the nature of
the redemption there is in Jesus.

*The Need:* When the old serpent—he who
had been cast out from heaven for his pride,
whose whole nature as the devil was pride—
spoke his words of temptation into the ear of
Eve, his words carried with them the very poi-

son of hell. And when she listened, and yielded her desire and her will to the prospect of being as God—knowing good and evil—the poison entered into her soul and blood and life. It destroyed forever that blessed humility and dependence on God which would have been our everlasting happiness. Instead of this, her life, and the life of the race that sprang from her, became corrupted to its very root with that most terrible of all sins and all curses—the poison of Satan's own pride.

All the wretchedness of which this world has been the scene has its origin in what this cursed, hellish pride, either our own, or that of others, has brought us. All wars and bloodshed among the nations, all selfishness and suffering, all ambitions and jealousies, all broken hearts and embittered lives, with all the daily unhappiness, are a result of this same wicked pride.

It is pride that made redemption needful. It is from our pride we need, above everything, to be redeemed. And our insight into the need of redemption will largely depend on our knowledge of the terrible nature of the power that has entered our being.

The power that Satan brought from hell and cast into man's life is working daily—hourly—with mighty power throughout the world. Men suffer from it; they fear and fight and flee it. But they still do not know where it comes from or from whom it gets its terrible power. No wonder they do not know where or how it is to be overcome.

Pride has its root and strength in a terrible spiritual power, outside of us as well as within us. We must confess it, deplore it, and be aware of its Satanic origin. This may lead us to despair of ever conquering it or casting it out. But it will also lead us all the sooner to that supernatural power in which alone our deliverance is to be found—the redemption of the Lamb of God. The hopeless struggle against the workings of self and pride within us may, indeed, become still more hopeless as we think of the power of darkness behind it all. But eventually, we will better realize and accept the power and life outside of ourselves—the humility of heaven, as brought down by the Lamb of God to cast out Satan and his pride.

Even as we need to look to the first Adam and his fall to know the power of the sin within us, we need to know well the Second Adam and His power to give within us a life of humility as real and abiding and overmastering as has been that of pride. We have our life from and in Christ, as truly, even more truly, than from and in Adam. We are to walk "rooted in Him," "holding fast the Head from which all the whole body increaseth with the increase of God" (Colossians 2:7, 19).

The life of God, which in the incarnation entered human nature, is the root in which we are to stand and grow. It is the same almighty power that worked there, and from then on to the resurrection, which works daily in us. Our one need is to study and know and trust the life that has been revealed in Christ as the life that is now ours. It waits for our consent to gain possession and mastery of our whole being.

In this view it is of inconceivable importance that we should have a correct understanding of who Christ is. We should properly comprehend what really constitutes Him, the Christ, and especially of what may be counted as His chief characteristic—the root and essence of all His character as our Redeemer. There can be only one answer: it is His humility. What is the incarnation but His heavenly humility, His emptying Himself and becoming man? What is His life on earth but humility, His taking the form of a servant? And what is His atonement but humility? "He humbled Himself and became obedient unto death." And what is His ascension and His glory, but humility exalted to the throne and crowned with glory? "He humbled Himself, wherefore God also hath highly exalted Him."

In heaven, where He was with the Father, in His birth, in His life, in His death, in His sitting on the throne, it is all, it is nothing, but humility. Christ is the humility of God embodied in human nature. He is the eternal love humbling itself, clothing itself in the garb of meekness and gentleness, to win and serve and save us. As the love and condescension of God makes Him the benefactor and helper and servant of all, so Jesus is and always will be the incarnate humility. Even in the midst of the throne, He is the meek and lowly Lamb of God.

If humility is the root of the tree, its nature must be seen in every branch, leaf, and fruit. If humility is the first, the all-inclusive grace of the life of Jesus, the secret of His atonement—then the health and strength of our spiritual life will entirely depend upon our putting this grace first, too. We must make humility the chief thing we admire in Him, the chief thing we ask of Him, the one thing for which we sacrifice all else. (See Note B.)

Is it any wonder that the Christian life is so often feeble and fruitless, when the very root of the Christ-life is neglected, is unknown? Is it any wonder that the joy of salvation is so little felt, when that in which Christ found it and brings it is so little sought? We must seek a humility which will rest in nothing less than the end and death of self; which gives up all the honor of men as Jesus did, to seek the honor that comes from God alone; which absolutely makes and counts itself nothing so that God may be all, that the Lord alone may be exalted. Until we seek humility in Christ above our chief joy, and welcome it at any price, there is very little hope of a religion that will conquer the world.

How much of the spirit of the meek and lowly Lamb of God do we see around us, in those who are called by His name? Think about how all the lack of love, the indifference to the needs, feelings, and weaknesses of others, the sharp and hasty judgments and utterances so often excused by our cries of being upright and honest, the manifestations of temper and irritation, the bitterness and estrangement, have their root in pride. Pride seeks only itself.

Devilish pride creeps in almost everywhere. What would happen if believers were to become permanently guided by the humility of Jesus? Oh, for the humility of Jesus in myself and everyone around me! We must honestly fix our hearts on our own lack of the humility revealed in Christ's life. Only then will we begin to feel what Christ and His salvation truly are.

Believer! *study the humility of Jesus.* This is the secret, the hidden root of your redemption. Sink down into it more deeply day by day. Believe with your whole heart that Christ—whom God has given us—will work in us, making us what the Father wants us to be.

## Chapter 3

# HUMILITY IN THE LIFE
# OF JESUS

*"I am among you as he that serveth"*—Luke 22:27.

In the Gospel of John, the inner life of our Lord becomes open to us. Jesus speaks frequently of His relationship to the Father, of the motives by which He is guided, and of His consciousness of the power and spirit in which He acts. Though the word *humble* is not written, there is no other place in Scripture where His humility is so clearly revealed.

We have already said that this grace is, in truth, nothing but man's simple consent to let God be all, in virtue of which he surrenders himself to His working alone. In Jesus we will see how both as the Son of God in heaven, and as man on earth, He took the place of entire subordination. He gave God the honor and the glory which is due to Him. And what He taught so often was made true to Himself: "He that humbleth himself shall be exalted" (Luke 18:14). As it is written, "He humbled Himself, wherefore God also hath highly exalted Him" (Philippians 2:8-9).

Listen to the words from John's Gospel, in which our Lord speaks of His relationship to the Father, and see how unceasingly He uses the words *not*, and *nothing*, of Himself. The *not I*, in which Paul expresses his relationship to Christ, is the very spirit of what Christ says of His relationship to the Father.

"The Son can do *nothing* of Himself" (John 5:19).

"I can of My own self do *nothing*; My judgment is just, because I seek *not* Mine own will" (John 5:30).

"I receive *not* honor from men" (John 5:41).

"I came down from heaven, *not* to do Mine own will" (John 6:38).

"My doctrine is *not* Mine" (John 7:16).

"I am *not* come of Myself" (John 7:28).

"I do *nothing* of Myself" (John 8:28).

"Neither came I of Myself, but He sent Me" (John 8:42).

"I seek *not* Mine own glory" (John 8:50).

"The words that I speak unto you, I speak *not* from Myself" (John 14:10).

"The word which ye hear is *not* Mine" (John 14:24).

These words open to us the deepest roots of

Christ's life and work. They tell us how it was that the Almighty God was able to work His mighty redemptive work through Him. They show how important Christ counted the state of heart which became Him as the Son of the Father. They teach us what the essential nature and life is of that redemption which Christ accomplished and now communicates.

Christ was nothing, that God might be all. He resigned Himself with His will and His powers entirely for the Father to work in Him. Of His own power, His own will, and His own glory, of His whole mission with all His works and His teaching, He said, "It is not I; I am nothing; I have given Myself to the Father to work. I am nothing, the Father is all."

Christ found this life of entire self-renunciation, of absolute submission and dependence upon the Father's will, to be one of perfect peace and joy. He lost nothing by giving everything to God. The Father honored His trust and did all for Him, and then exalted Him to His own right hand in glory. And because Christ had thus humbled Himself before God, and God was ever before Him, He found it possible to humble Himself before men, too. He was able to be the Servant of all. His humility was simply the surrender of Himself to God, to allow the Father to do in Him what He pleased, no matter what men around might say of Him, or do to Him.

It is in this state of mind, in this spirit and disposition, that the redemption of Christ has its virtue and effectiveness. It is to bring us to this disposition that we are made partakers of Christ. This is the true self-denial to which our Savior calls us—the acknowledgment that self has nothing good in it except as an empty vessel which God must fill. And also that its claim to be or do anything may not for a moment be allowed. It is in this, above and before everything, in which the conformity to Jesus consists. It is the being and doing nothing by ourselves so that God may be all.

Here we have the root and nature of true humility. It is because this is not understood or sought after that our humility is so superficial and so feeble. We must learn of Jesus, how He is meek and lowly of heart. He teaches us where true humility takes its rise and finds its strength—in the knowledge that it is God who works all in all, that our place is to yield to Him in perfect resignation and dependence, in full consent to be and to do nothing of ourselves. This is the life Christ came to reveal and to impart—a life in God that comes through death to sin and self.

If we feel that this life is too high for us and beyond our reach, it must, even more, urge us to seek it in Him. It is the indwelling Christ who will live this life in us, meek and lowly. If we long for this, let us, above everything, seek the holy secret of the knowledge of the nature of God as He every moment works all in all. The secret—of which all nature and every person and, above all, every child of God, is to be the witness—that he is nothing but a vessel, a channel, through which the living God can manifest the riches of His wisdom, power, and goodness. The root of all virtue and grace—of all faith and acceptable worship—is that we know that we have nothing but what we receive, and bow in deepest humility to wait upon God for it.

It was because this humility was not only a temporary sentiment—wakened up and brought into exercise when He thought of God—but the very spirit of His whole life, that Jesus was just as humble in His fellowship with men as with the Father. He counted Himself the Servant of God for the men whom God made and loved. As a natural consequence, He counted Himself the Servant of men, that through Him the Father might do His work of love. He never for a moment thought of seeking His honor, or asserting His power to vindicate Himself. His whole spirit was that of a life yielded to God that He might work in it. It is not until Christians study the humility of Jesus as the very essence of His redemption, and as the very blessedness of the life of the Son of God, that the void which should be filled with humility becomes a burden. It is not until they study His humility as the only true relationship to the Father, and therefore as that which Jesus must give us if we are to have any part with Him, that the terrible lack of actual, heavenly, manifest humility will become a sorrow. Our ordinary religion should be set aside to secure this, the first and the chief of the marks of Christ within us.

Brother or sister, are you clothed with humility? Ask your daily life. Ask Jesus. Ask your friends. Ask the world. And begin to praise God that there is opened up to you in Jesus a heavenly humility of which you have hardly known, and through which a heavenly blessedness (which you possibly have never yet tasted) can come into you.

## Chapter 4

# HUMILITY IN THE TEACHING
# OF JESUS

*"Learn of Me, for I am meek and lowly in heart"*—Matthew 11:29.

*"Whoseover will be chief among you, let him be your servant, even as the Son of Man came to serve"*—Matthew 20:27-28.

We have seen humility in the life of Christ as He laid open His heart to us. Let us listen to His teaching. There we will hear how He speaks of it, and how far He expects men, and especially His disciples, to be as humble as He was. Let us carefully study the passages, which I can scarce do more than quote, to receive the full impression of how often and how earnestly He taught it. It may help us to realize what He asks of us.

1. Look at the commencement of His ministry. In the Beatitudes with which the Sermon on the Mount opens, He speaks: *"Blessed are the poor in spirit; for theirs is the kingdom of heaven. Blessed are the meek; for they shall*

*inherit the earth"* (Matthew 5:3, 5). The very first words of His proclamation of the Kingdom of heaven reveal the open gate through which alone we enter. The poor, who have nothing in themselves, to them the Kingdom comes. The meek, who seek nothing in themselves, theirs will be the earth. The blessings of heaven and earth are for the lowly. For the heavenly and the earthly life, humility is the secret of blessing.

2. *"Learn of Me; for I am meek and lowly of heart, and ye shall find rest unto your souls"* (Matthew 11:29). Jesus offers Himself as Teacher. He tells us what the spirit is, which we will find in Him as Teacher, and which we can learn and receive from Him. Meekness and lowliness is the one thing He offers us; in it we will find perfect rest of soul. Humility is to be our salvation.

3. The disciples had been disputing who would be the greatest in the Kingdom, and had agreed to ask the Master (Luke 9:46; Matthew 18:3). He set a child in their midst, and said, *"Whosoever therefore shall humble himself as this little child, the same is greatest in the kingdom of heaven"*(Matthew 18:4). The question is indeed a far-reaching one. What will be the chief distinction in the heavenly Kingdom? The answer, none but Jesus would have given. The chief glory of heaven, the true heavenly-mindedness, the chief of the graces is humility.

*"He that is least among you, all the same shall be great"* (Luke 9:48).

4. The sons of Zebedee had asked Jesus to sit on His right and left, the highest place in the Kingdom. Jesus said it was not His to give, but the Father's, who would give it to those for whom it was prepared. They must not look or ask for it. Their thought must be of the cup and the baptism of humiliation. And then He added, *"Whosoever will be chief among you, let him be your servant. Even as the Son of Man came to serve."* Humility, as it is the mark of Christ the heavenly, will be the one standard of glory in heaven. The lowliest is the nearest to God. The prime position in the Church is promised to the humblest.

5. Speaking to the multitude and the disciples about the Pharisees and their love of the chief seats, Christ said once again (Matthew 12:11), *"He that is greatest among you shall be your servant."* Humiliation is the only ladder to honor in God's Kingdom.

6. On another occasion, in the house of a Pharisee, He spoke the parable of the guest who would be invited to come up higher (Luke 14:1-11), and added, *"For whosoever exalteth himself shall be abased; and he that humbleth himself shall be exalted."* The demand is inalterable; there is no other way. Self-abasement alone will be exalted.

7. After the parable of the Pharisee and the Publican, Christ spoke again (Luke 18:14), *"Everyone that exalteth himself shall be abased; and he that humbleth himself shall be exalted."* In the temple and presence and worship of God, everything is worthless that is not pervaded by deep, true humility toward God and men.

8. After washing the disciples' feet, Jesus said (John 13:14), *"If I then, the Lord and Master, have washed your feet, ye also ought to wash one another's feet."* The authority of command, example, and every thought, either of obedience or conformity, make humility the first and most essential element of discipleship.

9. At the Last Supper table, the disciples still disputed who should be greatest (Luke 22:26-27), and Jesus said, *"He that is greatest among you, let him be as the younger; and he that is chief, as he that doth serve. I am among you as he that serveth."* The path in which Jesus walked, and which He opened up for us, the power and spirit in which He brought about salvation, and to which He saves us, is the humility that always makes me the servant of all.

How little this is preached. How little it is practiced. How little the lack of it is felt or confessed. I do not say, how few attain to some recognizable measure of likeness to Jesus in His humility. But how few ever think of making it a distinct object of continual desire or prayer. How little the world has seen it. How little has it been seen even in the inner circle of the Church.

"Whosoever will be chief among you, let him be your servant." God wants us to believe that Jesus means this! We all know what the character of a faithful servant or slave implies. Devotion to the master's interests, thoughtful study and care to please him, delight in his prosperity and honor and happiness. There are servants on earth in whom these dispositions have been seen, and to whom the name of servant has never been anything but a glory.

To many of us it has been a new joy in the Christian life to know that we may yield ourselves as servants, as slaves to God, and to find that His service is our highest liberty—the liberty from sin and self. We need now to learn another lesson—that Jesus calls us to be servants of one another, and that, as we accept it heartily, this service too will be a most blessed one. It will be a new and fuller liberty from sin and self. At first it may appear hard; this is only because of the pride which still counts itself something.

If once we learn that to be nothing before God is the glory of man, the spirit of Jesus, the joy of heaven, we will welcome with our whole heart the discipline we may have in serving even those who try to vex us. When our own heart is set upon this, the true sanctification, we will study each word of Jesus on humility with new zest, and no place will be too low. No stooping will be too deep, and no service too mean or too long continued, if we may but share and prove the fellowship with Him who spoke, "I am among you as he that serveth" (Luke 22:27).

Brethren, here is the path to the higher life. Down, lower down! This was what Jesus always said to the disciples who were thinking of being great in the Kingdom, and of sitting on His right hand and His left. Seek not, ask not for exaltation; that is God's work. See to it that you abase and humble yourselves, and take no place before God or man but that of servant. That is your work, and let that also be your one purpose and prayer. God is faithful. Just as water always seeks and fills the lowest place, so the moment God finds men abased and empty, His glory and power flow in to exalt and to bless. He that humbles himself—that must be our one care—will be exalted; that is God's care. By His mighty power and in His great love He will do it.

Men sometimes speak as if humility and meekness would rob us of what is noble and bold and manlike. Oh, that all would believe that this is the nobility of the Kingdom of heaven! If they would only understand that this is the royal spirit that the King of heaven displayed, that this is God-like, to humble oneself, to become the servant of all! This is the path to the joy and the glory of Christ's presence ever in us, His power ever resting on us.

Jesus, the meek and lowly One, calls us to learn from Him the path to God. Let us study the words we have been reading, until our heart is filled with the thought: My one need is humility. And let us believe that what He shows, He gives; what He is, He imparts. As the meek and lowly One, He will come in and dwell in the longing heart.

Chapter 5

# HUMILITY IN THE DISCIPLES OF JESUS

*"Let he that is chief among you be as he that doth serve"*—Luke 22:26.

We have studied humility in the person and teaching of Jesus. Let us now look for it in the circle of His chosen companions—the twelve apostles. If we find a lack of it in them, then the contrast between Christ and men will be brought out more clearly, and it will help us to appreciate the mighty change which Pentecost worked in them. It will prove how real our participation can be in the perfect triumph of Christ's humility over the pride Satan had breathed into man.

In the texts quoted from the teaching of Jesus, we have already seen what the occasions were on which the disciples had proved how entirely lacking they were in the grace of humility. Once, they had been disputing about which of them should be the greatest. Another time, the sons of Zebedee, with their mother, had asked for the first places—the seat on the right hand and the left. And, later on, at the Supper table on the last night, there was again a contention over which should be accounted the greatest.

Not that there were not moments when they indeed humbled themselves before their Lord. So it was with Peter when he cried out, "Depart from me; for I am a sinful man, O Lord" (Luke 5:8). So, too, with the disciples when they fell down and worshipped Him who had stilled the storm. But such occasional expressions of humility only bring out into stronger relief what was the habitual tone of their mind. This tone was shown in the natural and spontaneous revelation, cited at other times, of the place and the power of self. The study of the meaning of all this will teach us several most important lessons.

First, *How much there may be of earnest and active Christianity while humility is still sadly wanting.* See it in the disciples. There was in them fervent attachment to Jesus. They had forsaken all for Him. The Father had revealed to them that He was the Christ of God. They believed in Him; they loved Him; they obeyed His commandments. They had forsaken all to follow Him. When others went back, they clung to Him. They were ready to die with Him. But deeper down than all this there was a dark power—the existence and the hideousness of which they were hardly conscious—which had to be slain and cast out before they could be the witnesses of the power of Jesus to save.

It is still the same today. We may find professors and ministers, evangelists and workers, missionaries and teachers, in whom the gifts of the Spirit are many and manifest, lacking in the grace of humility. There are those who are the channels of blessing to multitudes, but of whom—when the testing time comes, or closer fellowship gives fuller knowledge—it is only too painfully manifest that the abiding characteristic of the grace of humility is scarcely to be seen. All this tends to confirm the lesson that humility is one of the chief and the highest graces. It is one of the most difficult to attain, and one to which our first and greatest efforts ought to be directed. It is a grace that only comes in power, when the fullness of the Spirit makes us partakers of the indwelling Christ, and He lives within us.

Second, *How weak all external teaching and all personal effort is, to conquer pride or give the meek and lowly heart.* For three years the disciples had been in the training school of Jesus. He had told them that the chief lesson He wished to teach them was: "Learn of Me, for I am meek and lowly in heart" (Matthew 11:29).

37

Time after time He had spoken to them, to the Pharisees, to the multitude, about humility as the only path to the glory of God. He had not only lived before them as the Lamb of God in His divine humility, He had more than once unfolded to them the innermost secret of His life: "The Son of Man came not to be ministered unto, but to minister"; "I am among you as He that serveth" (Mark 10:45; Luke 22:27).

He had washed their feet, and told them they were to follow His example. And yet all had learned little. At the Last Supper there was still the contention as to who should be greatest. Doubtless, they had often tried to learn His lessons and firmly resolved not to grieve Him again. But all in vain. To teach them and us the much-needed lesson that no outward instruction, not even of Christ Himself—no argument, however convincing; no sense of the beauty of humility, however deep; no personal resolve or effort, however sincere and earnest—can cast out the devil of pride. When Satan casts out Satan, it is only to enter again in a mightier, though more hidden, power. Nothing can avail but that the new nature, in its divine humility, will be revealed in power to take the place of the old. It will become as truly our very nature as the old ever was.

Third, *It is only by the indwelling of Christ in His divine humility that we become truly hum-*

38

*ble.* We have our pride from another, from Adam; we must have our humility from another, too. Pride is ours, and rules in us with such terrible power, because it is ourself—our very nature. Humility must be ours in the same way; it must be our very self, our very nature. As natural and easy as it has been to be proud, it must be—it will be—to be humble. The promise is, "Where," even in the heart, "sin abounded, grace did much more abound" (Romans 5:20). All Christ's teaching of His disciples, and all their vain efforts, were the needful preparation for His entering into them in divine power—to give and be in them what He had taught them to desire.

In His death, Christ destroyed the power of the devil; He put away sin, and effected an everlasting redemption. In His resurrection, He received from the Father an entirely new life. It was a life of man in the power of God, capable of being communicated to men, and entering, renewing, and filling their lives with His divine power. In His ascension, He received the Spirit of the Father, through whom He might do what He could not do while on earth. Then He was able to make Himself one with those He loved, and actually live their life for them, so that they could live before the Father in a humility like His, because it was He Himself who lived and breathed in them. And on Pentecost, He came and took possession. The work of preparation and conviction, the awakening of desire and hope which His teaching had effected, was perfected by the mighty change that Pentecost brought about. And the lives and the Epistles of James and Peter and John bear witness that all was changed, and that the spirit of the meek and suffering Jesus indeed had possession of them.

What will we say to these things? I am sure there is more than one class among my readers. There may be some who have never yet thought very much of the matter, and cannot at once realize its immense importance as a life question for the Church and its every member. There are others who have felt condemned for their shortcomings and have put forth very earnest efforts, only to fail and be discouraged. Others, again, may be able to give joyful testimony of spiritual blessing and power, and yet there has never been the needed conviction of what those around them still see as lacking. And still others may be able to witness that in regard to this grace, too, the Lord has given deliverance and victory, while He has taught them how much they still need and may expect out of the fullness of Jesus.

To whichever class we belong, may I urge the pressing need there is for each of us to seek a still deeper conviction of the unique place that humility holds in becoming like Christ. We must understand the utter impossibility of the

Church or the believer in being what Christ would have them be, as long as *His humility is not recognized as His chief glory, His first command, and our highest blessedness.* Let us deeply consider how far the disciples were advanced while this grace was still so terribly lacking. Let us pray to God that other gifts may not so satisfy us that we never grasp the fact that the absence of this grace is the secret reason why the power of God cannot do its mighty work. It is only where we, like the Son, truly know and show that we can do nothing of ourselves, that God will do all.

It is when the truth of an indwelling Christ takes the place it claims in the experience of believers that the Church will put on her beautiful garments and humility will be seen in her teachers and members as the beauty of holiness.

## Chapter 6

## HUMILITY IN DAILY LIFE

*"He that loveth not his brother whom he hath seen, how can he love God whom he hath not seen?"*—1 John 4:20.

What a solemn thought, that our love to God will be measured by our everyday fellowship with men and the love it displays. How solemn that our love to God will be found to be a delusion, except as its truth is proved in standing the test of daily life with our fellow-men. It is even so with our humility. It is easy to think we humble ourselves before God. Yet, humility toward men will be the only sufficient proof that our humility before God is real. It will be the only proof that humility has taken up its abode in us, and become our very nature—that we actually, like Christ, have made ourselves of no reputation. When in the presence of God lowliness of heart has become, not a posture we assume for a time when we think of Him, or pray to Him, but the very spirit of our life, it will manifest itself in all our bearing toward our brethren.

The lesson is one of deep importance. The only humility that is really ours is not that which we try to show before God in prayer, but that which we carry with us, and carry out, in our ordinary conduct. The insignificances of daily life are the importances and the tests of eternity because they prove what spirit really possesses us. It is in our most unguarded moments that we really show and see what we are. To know the humble man, to know how the humble man behaves, you must follow him in the common course of daily life.

Is this not what Jesus taught? He taught His lessons of humility when the disciples disputed who should be greatest, when He saw how the Pharisees loved the chief place at feasts and the chief seats in the synagogues, and when He had given them the example of washing their feet. Humility before God is nothing if not proved in humility before men.

It is even so in the teaching of Paul. To the Romans he writes: "In honor preferring *one another*"; "Mind not high things, but condescend to men of low estate. Be not wise in your own conceits" (Romans 12:10, 16). To the Corinthians: "Love," and there is no love without humility as its root, "vaunteth not itself, is not puffed up, seeketh not its own, is not provoked "(1 Corinthians 13:4-5). To the Galatians: "Through love serve *one another*"; "Let us not be desirous of vainglory, provoking *one another*, envying *one another*" (Galatians 5:13, 26). To the Ephesians, immediately after the three wonderful chapters on the heavenly life: "Therefore, walk with all lowliness and meekness, with long-suffering, forbearing *one another* in love"; "Giving thanks always, submitting yourselves *one to another* in the fear of God" (Ephesians 4:2; 5:20-21). To the Philippians: "Let nothing be done through strife or vainglory, but in lowliness of mind, let each esteem the *other* better than themselves"; "Let this mind be in you which was also in Christ Jesus: Who made Himself of no reputation, and took upon Him the form of a servant, and humbled Himself" (Philippians 2:3, 5, 7-8). And to the Colossians: "Put on a heart of compassion, kindness, humility, meekness, long-suffering, forebearing *one another*, and forgiving *one another*, even as Christ forgave you" (Colossians 3:12-13). It is in our relationship to one another, in our treatment of one another, that the true lowliness of mind and the humility of heart are to be seen. Our humility before God has no value, except that it prepares us to reveal the humility of Jesus to our fellow-men. Let us study humility in daily life in the light of these words.

The humble man seeks at all times to act on the rule, *"In honor preferring one another; Serve one another; Each esteeming others better than himself; Submitting yourselves one to another."* It is often asked—how can we count others better than ourselves, when we see that they are far below us in wisdom and in holiness, in natural gifts, or in grace received? The question proves at once how little we understand what real lowliness of mind is. True humility comes when, in the light of God, we have seen ourselves to be nothing, have consented to part with and cast away self—to let God be all. The soul that has done this and can say, "So have I lost myself in finding You," no longer compares itself with others. It has forever given up every thought of self in God's presence. It meets its fellow-man as one who is nothing, and seeks nothing for itself. It is a soul that serves God and, for His sake, serves all. A faithful servant may be wiser than the master, and yet retain the true spirit and posture of the servant. The humble man looks upon every child of God—even the feeblest and unworthiest—and honors him and prefers him in honor as the son of a King. The spirit of Him who washed the disciples' feet makes it a joy to us to be indeed the least, to be servants one of another.

The humble man feels no jealousy or envy. He

can praise God when others are preferred and blessed before him. He can bear to hear others praised and himself forgotten, because in God's presence he has learned to say with Paul, "I am nothing" (2 Corinthians 12:11). He has received the spirit of Jesus, who pleased not Himself and sought not His own honor, as the spirit of his life.

Amid what are considered the temptations to impatience and touchiness, to hard thoughts and sharp words—which come from the failings and sins of fellow-Christians—the humble man carries the often repeated injunction in his heart, and shows it in his life: *"Forbearing one another, and forgiving one another, even as Christ forgave you"* (Colossians 3:13). He has learned that in putting on the Lord Jesus he has *put on the heart of compassion, kindness, humility, meekness, and long-suffering* (Colossians 3:12). Jesus has taken the place of self, and it is not an impossibility to forgive as Jesus forgave. His humility does not consist merely in thoughts or words of self-depreciation, but, as Paul puts it, in "a heart of humility." It is a heart encompasssed by compassion and kindness, meekness and long-suffering—the sweet and lowly gentleness recognized as the mark of the Lamb of God.

In striving after the higher experiences of the Christian life, the believer is often in danger of aiming at and rejoicing in what one might call the more human virtues. Such virtues are boldness, joy, contempt of the world, zeal, self-sacrifice—even the old Stoics taught and practiced these. While the deeper and gentler, the more divine and heavenly graces are scarcely thought of or valued. These virtues are those which Jesus first taught upon earth—because He brought them from heaven—those which are more distinctly connected with His cross and the death of self—poverty of spirit, meekness, humility, lowliness. Therefore, let us put on a heart of compassion, kindness, humility, meekness, long-suffering. Let us prove our Christ-likeness, not only in our zeal for saving the lost, but before all in our dealings with the brethren, forbearing and forgiving one another, *even as the Lord forgave us*.

Fellow Christians, do let us study the Bible portrait of the humble man. And let us ask our brethren, and ask the world, whether they recognize in us the likeness to the original. Let us be content with nothing less than taking each of these texts as the promise of what God will work in us. Let us take them as the revelation in words of what the Spirit of Jesus will give as a birth within us. And let each failure and shortcoming simply urge us to turn humbly and meekly to the meek and lowly Lamb of God. Have full assurance that where He is enthroned in the heart,

His humility and gentleness will be one of the streams of living water that flow from within us.[1]

Once again I repeat what I have said before. I feel deeply that we have very little conception of what the Church suffers from the lack of this divine humility—the nothingness that makes room for God to prove His power. It is not long since a Christian, of a humble, loving spirit—acquainted with many mission stations of various societies—expressed his deep sorrow that in some cases the spirit of love and forbearance was sadly lacking. Men and women, brought close together with others of uncongenial minds, find it hard to bear and to love and to keep the unity of the Spirit in the bond of peace. And those who should have been fellow-helpers of each other's joy become a hindrance and a weariness. And all for one reason—the lack of the humility which counts itself nothing, which rejoices in becoming and being counted the least, and only seeks, like Jesus, to be the servant, the helper and comforter of others, even

---

[1]"I knew Jesus, and He was very precious to my soul: but I found something in me that would not keep sweet and patient and kind. I did what I could to keep it down, but it was there. I besought Jesus to do something for me, and when I gave Him my will, He came to my heart, and took out all that would not be sweet, all that would not be kind, all that would not be patient, and then He shut the door."— George Foxe.

the lowest and unworthiest.

And where does it come from, that men who have joyfully given themselves up for Christ find it so hard to give themselves up for their brethren? Is the Church not to blame? It has so little taught its sons that the humility of Christ is the first of the virtues, the best of all the graces and powers of the Spirit. The Church has so little proved that a Christ-like humility is what it, like Christ, places and preaches first, as what is needed and possible, too. But let us not be discouraged. Let the discovery of the lack of this grace stir us to larger expectation from God. Let us look on every brother or sister who tries or vexes us as God's means of grace. Let us look on him or her as God's instrument for our purification, for our exercise of the humility Jesus, our life, breathes within us. And let us have such faith in the all of God and the nothing of self, that we may, in God's power, seek only to serve one another in love.

## Chapter 7

## HUMILITY AND HOLINESS

*"Which say, Stand by thyself, come not near to me; for I am holier than thou"*—Isaiah 65:5.

We speak of the Holiness movement in our times, and praise God for it. We hear a great deal about seekers after holiness and professors of holiness, of holiness teaching and holiness meetings. The blessed truths of holiness in Christ, and holiness by faith, are being emphasized as never before. The great test of whether the holiness we profess to seek or to attain is truth and life will be *whether it produces an increasing humility in us*. In man, humility is the one thing needed to allow God's holiness to dwell in him and shine through him. In Jesus, the Holy One of God who makes us holy, a divine humility was the secret of His life, His death, and His exaltation. The one infallible test of our holiness will be the humility before God and men which marks us. Humility is the bloom

51

and the beauty of holiness.

The chief mark of counterfeit holiness is its lack of humility. Every seeker after holiness needs to be on his guard, so that, unconsciously, what was begun in the Spirit is not perfected in the flesh, and pride does not creep in where its presence is least expected. Two men went up into the temple to pray: the one a Pharisee, the other a publican. There is no place or position so sacred that the "Pharisee" can not enter. Pride can lift its head in the very temple of God, and make His worship the scene of its self-exaltation.

Since the time Christ so exposed his pride, the Pharisee has put on the garb of the publican. The confessor of deep sinfulness equally with the professor of the highest holiness, must be on the watch. Just when we are most anxious to have our heart be the temple of God, we will find the two men coming up to pray. And the publican will find that his danger is not from the Pharisee beside him, who despises him, but from the Pharisee within, who commends and exalts. In God's temple, when we think we are in the holiest of all, in the presence of His holiness, let us beware of pride. "Now there was a day when the sons of God came to present themselves before the Lord, and Satan came also among them" (Job 1:6).

"God, I thank thee, I am not as other men, or

even as this publican" (Luke 18:11). Self finds its cause of complacency in that which is just cause for thanksgiving, in the very thanksgiving which we render to God, and in the very confession that God has done it all. Yes, even in the temple, when the language of penitence and trust in God's mercy alone is heard, the Pharisee may take up the note of praise, and in thanking God be congratulating himself. Pride can clothe itself in the garments of praise or of penitence.

Even though the words, "I am not as other men" are rejected and condemned, their spirit may too often be found in our feelings and language toward our fellow-worshipers and fellow-men. If you want to know if this is really so, just listen to the way in which churches and Christians often speak of one another. How little of the meekness and gentleness of Jesus is to be seen. It is so little remembered that deep humility must be the keynote of what the servants of Jesus say of themselves or each other. Is there not many a church or assembly of the saints, many a mission or convention, many a society or committee, even many a mission away in heathendom, where the harmony has been disturbed and the work of God hindered? Is it not because men who are counted saints have proved in touchiness and haste and impatience, in self-defense and self-assertion, in sharp judgments and unkind words, that they did not each esteem others better than themselves? Is it not because their holiness has in it little of the meekness of the saints?[1]

In their spiritual history, men may have had times of great humbling and brokenness, but what a different thing this is from being clothed with humility, and from having a humble spirit. How different this is from having that lowliness of mind in which each counts himself the servant of others, and so shows forth the very mind which was also in Jesus Christ.

*"Stand by; for I am holier than thou!"* What a parody on holiness! Jesus the Holy One is the humble One. The holiest will always be the humblest. There is none holy but God. We have as much of holiness as we have of God. And according to what we have of God will be our real humility, because humility is nothing but the disappearance of self in the vision that God is all. The holiest will be the humblest. Alas! though the bare-faced boasting Jew of the days of Isaiah is not often to be found—even our manners have taught us not to speak thus—how often his spirit is still seen, whether in the treat-

[1]"Me is a most exacting personage, requiring the best seat and the highest place for itself, and feeling grievously wounded if its claim is not recognized. Most of the quarrels among Christian workers arise from the clamoring of this gigantic Me. How few of us understand the true secret of taking our seats in the lowest rooms."—Hannah Whitall Smith.

ment of fellow-saints or of the children of the world. In the spirit in which opinions are given, work is undertaken, and faults are exposed, how often, though the garb be that of the publican, the voice is still that of the Pharisee, "Oh God, I thank Thee that I am not as other men" (Luke 18:11).

And is there, then, any humility to be found that men will indeed still count themselves "less than the least of all saints" (Ephesians 3:8), the servants of all? There is. "Love vaunteth not itself, is not puffed up, seeketh not her own" (1 Corinthians 13:4-5). The power of a perfect love forgets itself and finds its blessedness in blessing others—in bearing with and honoring them, however feeble they may be. The power of this love is given where the spirit of love is shed abroad in the heart, where the divine nature comes to a full birth, and where Christ, the meek and lowly Lamb of God, is truly formed within. Where this love enters, there God enters. And where God has entered in His power, and reveals Himself as all, there man becomes nothing. And where man becomes nothing before God, he cannot be anything but humble toward his fellow-men. The presence of God becomes not a thing of times and seasons, but the covering under which the soul always dwells. Its deep humility before God becomes the holy place of His presence from which all its words and works proceed.

May God teach us that our thoughts and words and feelings concerning our fellow-men are His test of our humility toward Him. May He teach us that our humility before Him is the only power that can enable us to be always humble with our fellow-men. Our humility must be the life of Christ, the Lamb of God, within us.

Let all teachers of holiness, whether in the pulpit or on the platform, and all seekers after holiness, whether in the closet or in the convention, take warning. There is no pride so dangerous, none so subtle and insidious, as the pride of holiness. It is not that a man ever says, or even thinks, "Stand by; I am holier than thou." No, indeed, the thought would be regarded with abhorrence. But there grows up, all unconsciously, a hidden habit of soul which feels complacency in its attainments. It cannot help seeing how far it is in advance of others. It can be recognized, not always in any special self-assertion or self-laudation, but simply in the absence of that deep self-abasement which is the mark of the soul that has seen the glory of God (Job 42:5-6; Isaiah 6:5). It reveals itself, not only in words or thoughts, but in a tone—a way of speaking to others—in which those who have the gift of spiritual discernment cannot help but recognize the power of self. Even the world with its keen eyes notices it. The world points to it as a proof that the profession of a heavenly life does not bear any especially heavenly fruits.

Oh brethren! let us beware. Unless we make the increase of humility our study, we may find that we have been delighting in beautiful thoughts and feelings, in solemn acts of consecration and faith, while the only sure mark of the presence of God—the disappearance of self—was all the time wanting. Come and let us flee to Jesus, and hide ourselves in Him until we are clothed with His humility. That alone is our holiness.

.

## Chapter 8

## HUMILITY AND SIN

*"Sinners, of whom I am chief"*—1 Timothy
1:15.

Humility is often identified with penitence
and contrition. As a consequence, there appears
to be no way of fostering humility but by keep-
ing the soul occupied with its sin. We have
learned, I think, that humility is something else
and something more. We have seen in the teaching of our Lord Jesus and in the Epistles how
often the virtue is earnestly taught without any
reference to sin. In the very nature of things—in
the whole relationship of man to the Creator—
in the life of Jesus as He lived it and imparts it to
us, humility is the very essence of holiness and of
blessedness. It is the displacement of self by the
enthronement of God. Where God is all, self is
nothing.

Though it is this aspect of the truth I have felt
it especially needful to press, I hardly need to

say what new depth and intensity man's sin and God's grace give to the humility of the saints. We have only to look at a man like the Apostle Paul to see how, through his life as a ransomed and a holy man, the deep consciousness of having been a sinner lives inextinguishably.

We all know the passages in which Paul refers to his life as a persecutor and blasphemer. "I am *the least of the apostles*, that am *not fit to be called an apostle*, because I persecuted the Church of God...I labored more abundantly than they all; yet not I, but the grace of God which was with me" (1 Corinthians 15:9-10). "Unto me, who am *less than the least of all saints*, is this grace given, that I should preach among the Gentiles" (Ephesians 3:8). "I was before *a blasphemer, and a persecutor, and injurious;* but I obtained mercy, because I did it ignorantly in unbelief. ...Christ Jesus came into the world to save *sinners, of whom I am chief*" (1 Timothy 1:13-15).

God's grace had saved Paul; God remembered his sins no more; but never, never could he forget how terribly he had sinned. The more he rejoiced in God's salvation, and the more his experience of God's grace filled him with unspeakable joy, the clearer was his consciousness that he was a saved sinner. And he was more aware that salvation had no meaning or sweetness except as the sense of his being a sinner made it precious and real to him. Never for a moment could he forget that it was a sinner God had taken up in His arms and crowned with His love.

The texts we have just quoted are sometimes referred to as Paul's confession of daily sinning. One has only to read them carefully in their connection to see how little this is the case. They have a far deeper meaning. They refer to that which lasts throughout eternity, and which will give its deep undertone of amazement and adoration to the humility with which the ransomed bow before the throne, as those who have been washed from their sins by the blood of the Lamb. Never, never, even in glory, can they be other than ransomed sinners. Never for a moment in this life can God's child live in the full light of His love without understanding that the sin out of which he has been saved is his one only right and title to all that grace has promised to do.

The humility with which he first came as a sinner acquires a new meaning when he learns how it becomes him as a man. And then ever again, the humility in which he was born as a man has its deepest, richest tones of adoration in the memory of what it is to be a monument of God's wondrous, redeeming love.

The true import of what these expressions of St. Paul teach us comes out all the more strongly when we notice the remarkable fact that, through his whole Christian course, we never find anything like a confession of sin. Not even in the Epistles where he expounds on the most intensely personal unbosomings does he confess his sins. Nowhere is there any mention of shortcoming or defect, nowhere any suggestion to his readers that he has failed in duty, or sinned against the law of perfect love.

On the contrary, there are many passages in which he vindicates himself in language that means nothing if it does not appeal to a faultless life before God and men. "Ye are witnesses, and God also, how holily, and justly, and unblameably we behaved ourselves among you that believe "(1 Thessalonians 2:10). "Our rejoicing is this, the testimony of our conscience, that in simplicity and godly sincerity we have had our conversation in the world, and more abundantly to you-ward" (2 Corinthians 1:12). This is not an ideal or an aspiration. It is an appeal to what his actual life had been. However we may account for this absence of confession of sin, all will admit that it must point to a life in the power of the Holy Spirit, such as is but seldom realized or expected in our days.

The point which I wish to emphasize is this— the very fact of the absence of such confession of sinning only gives more force to the truth that it is not in daily sinning that the secret of the deeper humility will be found. But, it is to be found in the habitual, never for a moment to be forgotten position, which the more abundant grace will keep more distinctly alive. It is that our true place—the only place of blessing, our one abiding position before God—must be that of those whose highest joy is to confess that they are sinners saved by grace.

Coupled with Paul's deep remembrance of having sinned so terribly in the past, before grace and the consciousness of being kept from present sinning had met him, was the abiding remembrance of the dark, hidden power of sin ever ready to come in, and only kept out by the presence and power of the indwelling Christ. "In me, that is, in my flesh, dwelleth no good thing" (Romans 7:18). These words describe the flesh as it is to the end. "The law of the Spirit of life in Christ Jesus hath now made me free from the law of sin and death" (Romans 8:2). This glorious deliverance is neither the annihilation nor the sanctification of the flesh, but a continuous victory given by the Spirit as He mortifies the deeds of the body.

As health expels disease, and light swallows up darkness, and life conquers death, the indwelling of Christ through the Spirit is the health and light and life of the soul. But with this, the conviction of our helplessness and danger always tempers our faith in this momentary and unbroken action of the Holy Spirit, giving us a chastened sense of dependence and making faith and joy the handmaids of humility. This humility lives only by the grace of God.

The three passages quoted above all show that it was the wonderful grace bestowed upon Paul, and of which he felt the need every moment, that humbled him so deeply. The grace of God that was with him enabled him to labor more abundantly than the others. The very nature and glory of grace for the sinner is the grace to preach to the heathen the unsearchable riches of Christ. It is also the grace that was exceedingly abundant with the faith and love which is in Christ Jesus. It was this grace which kept Paul's consciousness of having once sinned, and being liable to sin, so intensely alive. "Where sin abounded, grace did much more abound" (Romans 5:20). This reveals how the very essence of grace is to deal with and take away sin, and how it must always be so. The more abundant the experience of grace, the more intense the consciousness of being a sinner. It is not sin, but God's grace showing a man and constantly reminding him what a sinner he was, that will keep him truly humble. It is not sin, but grace, that will make me indeed know myself as a sinner, and make the sinner's place of deepest humility the place I never leave.

I fear that there are many who have sought to humble themselves by strong expressions of self-condemnation and self-denunciation, and yet have to confess with sorrow that a humble spirit, accompanied by kindness, compassion, meekness, and forbearance, is still as far off as ever. Being occupied with self, even amid the deepest self-abhorrence, can never free us from self. It is the revelation of God, not only by the law condemning sin, but by His grace delivering from it, that will make us humble. The law may break the heart with fear. But it is only grace that works that sweet humility which becomes a joy to the soul as its second nature. It was the revelation of God in His holiness, drawing near to make Himself known in His grace, that made Abraham and Jacob, Job and Isaiah, bow so low. There will be no room for self in the soul that waits for, trusts, worships, and is filled with the presence of God the Creator as the all of man in his nothingness, and God the Redeemer as the all of the sinner in his sinfulness. In only this way can the promise be fulfilled: "The haughtiness of man shall be made low, and the Lord alone be exalted in that day" (Isaiah 2:17).

It is the sinner dwelling in the full light of God's holy, redeeming love—in the experience of that full indwelling of divine love, which comes through Christ and the Holy Spirit—

who cannot be anything but humble. Not to be occupied with your sin, but to be occupied with God, brings deliverance from self.

Chapter 9

## HUMILITY AND FAITH

*"How can ye believe, which rather honor one of another, and seek not the honor that cometh from God only?"*—John 5:44.

In an address I heard lately, the speaker said that the blessings of the higher Christian life were often like the objects exposed in a shop window— one could see them clearly and yet could not reach them. If told to stretch out his hand and take, a man would answer, "I cannot; there is a thick pane of plate glass between me and them." Likewise, Christians may clearly see the blessed promises of perfect peace and rest, of overflowing love and joy, of abiding communion and fruitfulness, yet feel that there is something in-between hindering the true possession. And what might that be? *Nothing but pride.*

The promises made to faith are so free and sure, the invitations and encouragements are so strong, and the mighty power of God on which it may count is so near and free, that only something which hinders faith can hinder the blessing from being ours. In our text, Jesus discloses to us that it is indeed pride which makes faith impossible. "How can ye believe, which rather honor one of another?" As we see how, in their very nature, pride and faith are irreconcilably at variance, we will learn that faith and humility are at root one. We will learn that we can never have more of true faith than we have of true humility. We will see that we may indeed have strong intellectual conviction and assurance of the truth while pride is kept in the heart, but that it makes the living faith—which has power with God—an impossibility.

We need only think for a moment what faith is. Is it not the confession of nothingness and helplessness, the surrender and the waiting to let God work? Is it not in itself the most humbling thing there can be—the acceptance of our place as dependents, who can claim or get or do nothing but what grace bestows? Humility is simply the disposition which prepares the soul for living on trust. And every, even the most secret breathing of pride—in self-seeking, self-will, self-confidence, or self-exaltation—is just the strengthening of that self which cannot enter into the Kingdom or possess the things of the Kingdom, because it refuses to allow God to be what He is and must be—the all in all.

Faith is the organ or sense for the perception and apprehension of the heavenly world and its blessings. Faith seeks the glory that comes from God—that only comes where God is all. As long as we take glory from one another, as long as we seek and love and jealously guard the glory of this life—the honor and reputation that comes from men—we do not seek and cannot receive the glory that comes from God. Pride renders faith impossible. Salvation comes through a cross and a crucified Christ. Salvation is the fellowship with the crucified Christ in the Spirit of His cross. Salvation is union with, delight and participation in, the humility of Jesus. Is it any wonder that our faith is so feeble when pride still reigns so much, and we have hardly learned to long or pray for humility as the most needful and blessed part of salvation?

Humility and faith are more nearly allied in Scripture than many know. See it in the life of Christ. There are two cases in which He spoke of a great faith. In the first instance, the centurion said, "I am not worthy that Thou shouldst come under my roof." At this humility, Jesus marveled and replied, "I have not found so great faith, no, not in Israel" (Matthew 8:8, 10). In the second case, the mother humbly spoke, "Truth, Lord, yet the dogs eat of the crumbs." And the Lord answered her, "O woman, great is thy faith!" (Matthew 15:27-28). It is the humility that brings a soul to be nothing before God that also removes every hindrance to faith. Humility makes the soul fear that it would dishonor Him by not trusting Him wholly.

Brethren, have we not here the cause of failure in the pursuit of holiness? Is it not this that made our consecration and our faith so superficial and so short-lived? We had no idea to what an extent pride and self were still secretly working within us. We were not aware of how God alone, by His incoming and His mighty power, could cast them out. We did not understand how nothing but the new and divine nature, entirely taking the place of the old self, could make us really humble. We did not know that absolute, unceasing, universal humility must be the root disposition of every prayer and every approach to God, as well as of every dealing with man. We did not realize that we might as well attempt to see without eyes, or live without breath, as believe or draw near to God or rest in His love, without an all-prevading humility and lowliness of heart.

Brethren, have we not been making a mistake in taking so much trouble to believe, while all the time there was the old self in its pride seeking to possess itself of God's blessing and riches? No wonder we could not believe. Let us change our course. Let us seek first of all to humble ourselves under the mighty hand of God: *He will exalt us.* The cross, the death, and the grave, into which Jesus humbled Himself, were His path to the glory of God. And they are our path. Let our one desire and our fervent prayer be to be humbled with Him and like Him. Let us gladly accept whatever can humble us before God or men—this alone is the path to the glory of God.

You perhaps feel inclined to ask a question. I have spoken of some who have blessed experiences, or are the means of bringing blessing to others, and yet are lacking in humility. You ask whether these do not prove that they have true, strong faith, even though they all too clearly seek the honor that comes from men.

More than one answer can be given. But the principal answer in our present connection is this—they indeed have a measure of faith, in proportion to which, and with the special gifts bestowed upon them, is the blessing they bring to others. But in that very blessing, the work of their faith is hindered through the lack of humility. The blessing is often superficial or transitory just because they are not the nothing that opens the way for God to be all. A deeper humility would, without doubt, bring a deeper and fuller blessing. The Holy Spirit not only working in them as a Spirit of power, but dwelling in them in the fullness of His grace—especially that of humility— would communicate Himself through them for a life of power, holiness and steadfastness now seen all too little.

"How can ye believe, which rather honor one of another?" Brethren! nothing can cure you of the desire to receive honor from men, or of the sensitivity and pain and anger which come when it is not given, except giving yourself to seek only the glory that comes from God. Let the glory of the all-glorious God be everything to you. You will be freed from the glory of men and of self, and be content and glad to be nothing. Out of this nothingness you will grow strong in faith, giving glory to God. You will find that the deeper you sink in humility before Him, the nearer He is to fulfill every desire of your faith.

## Chapter 10

## HUMILITY AND DEATH TO SELF

*"He humbled Himself and became obedient unto death"*—Philippians 2:8.

Humility is the path to death, because in death it gives the highest proof of its perfection. Humility is the blossom of which death to self is the perfect fruit. Jesus humbled Himself unto death and opened the path in which we too must walk. As there was no way for Him to prove His surrender to God to the very uttermost, or to give up and rise out of His human nature to the glory of the Father, but through death, so it is with us, too. Humility must lead us to die to self. We must prove how wholly we have given ourselves up to it and to God. Only thus are we freed from fallen nature and find the path that leads to life in God, to that full birth of the new nature of which humility is the breath and the joy.

We have spoken of what Jesus did for His

disciples when He communicated His resurrection life to them. In the descent of the Holy Spirit, He, the glorified and enthroned meekness, actually came from heaven Himself to dwell in them. He won the power to do this through death; in its inmost nature the life He imparts is a life out of death. It is a life that has been surrendered to death and been won through death. He who came to dwell in them was Himself One who had been dead and now lives forevermore. His life, His person, His presence, bears the marks of death, of being a life begotten out of death.

That life in His disciples bears the death-marks, too. It is only as the Spirit of the death, of the dying One, dwells and works in the soul, that the power of His life can be known. The first and chief of the marks of the dying of the Lord Jesus—the death-marks that show the true follower of Jesus—is humility. For these two reasons, only humility leads to perfect death. Only death perfects humility. Humility and death are in their very nature one. Humility is the bud; in death the fruit is ripened to perfection.

*Humility leads to perfect death.* Humility means the giving up of self and becoming perfect nothingness before God. Jesus humbled Himself and became obedient unto death. In death He gave the highest, the perfect proof of having given up His will to the will of God. In death He gave up His self, with its natural reluctance to drink the cup. He gave up the life He had in union with our human nature. He died to self and the sin that tempted Him, so, as man, He entered into the perfect life of God. If it had not been for His boundless humility, counting Himself as nothing except as a servant to do and suffer the will of God, He would never have died.

This gives us the answer to the question so often asked, and of which the meaning is so seldom clearly apprehended: How can I die to self? The death to self is not your work; it is God's work. In Christ *you are dead* to sin. The life there is in you has gone through the process of death and resurrection. You may be sure you are indeed dead to sin. But the full manifestation of the power of this death in your disposition and conduct depends on the measure in which the Holy Spirit imparts the power of the death of Christ. And it is here that the teaching is needed. If you want to enter into full fellowship with Christ in His death, and know the full deliverance from self, humble yourself. This is your one duty.

Place yourself before God in your utter helplessness. Consent heartily to the fact of your weakness to slay or make yourself alive. Sink down into your own nothingness, in the spirit of meek and patient and trustful surrender to God. Accept every humiliation, look upon every fellow-man who tries or vexes you, as a means of grace to humble you. Use every opportunity of humbling yourself before your fellow-men as a help to remain humble before God. It is by the mighty strengthening of His Holy Spirit that God reveals Christ fully in you. In this manner, Christ, in His form of a servant, is truly formed in you and dwells in your heart. God will accept such humbling of yourself as the proof that your whole heart desires it. He will accept it as your very best prayer for it, and as your preparation for His mighty work of grace. It is the path of humility which leads to perfect death, the full and perfect experience that we are dead in Christ.

Then follows: *Only this death leads to perfect humility*. Oh, beware of the mistake so many make, who would like to be humble, but are afraid to be too humble. They have so many qualifications and limitations, so many reasonings and questionings, as to what true humility is to be and to do, that they never unreservedly yield themselves to it. Beware of this. Humble yourself unto the death. It is in the death to self that humility is perfected. Be sure that at the root of all real experience of more grace, of all true advance in consecration, of all actually increasing conformity to the likeness of Jesus, there must be a deadness to self that proves itself to God and men in our dispositions and habits.

It is sadly possible to speak of the death-life and the Spirit-walk, while even the tenderest love sees how much there is of self. The death to self has no surer death-mark than a humility which makes no reputation of itself, which empties out self and takes the form of a servant. It is possible to speak much and honestly of fellowship with a despised and rejected Jesus, and of bearing His cross, while the meek, lowly, kind, and gentle humility of the Lamb of God is not seen—is scarcely sought. The Lamb of God means two things—meekness and death. Let us seek to receive Him in both forms. In Him they are inseparable; they must be in us also.

What a hopeless task if we had to do the work! Nature can never overcome nature, not even with the help of grace. Self can never cast out self, even in the regenerate man. Praise God! the work has been done, finished and perfected forever. The death of Jesus, once and forever, is our death to self. And the ascension of Jesus, His entering once and forever into the Holiest, has given us the Holy Spirit to communicate to us in power, and makes the power of the death-life our very own. As the soul, in the pursuit and practice of humility, follows in the steps of Jesus, its consciousness of the need of something more is awakened. Its desire and hope is quickened; its faith is strengthened; and it learns to look up and claim and receive that true fullness of the Spirit of Jesus. That fullness can daily maintain His death to self and sin in its full power, and make humility the all-pervading spirit of our life. (See Note C.)

"Know ye not, that so many of us as were baptized into Jesus Christ were *baptized into His death?* Likewise reckon ye also to be *dead indeed unto sin*, but alive unto God through Jesus Christ our Lord. Yield yourselves unto God, as *alive from the dead"* (Romans 6:3, 11, 13). The whole self-consciousness of the Christian is to be imbued and characterized by the Spirit that animated the death of Christ. He has to ever present himself to God as one who has died in Christ, and in Christ is alive from the dead, bearing about in his body the dying of the Lord Jesus. His life ever bears the two-fold mark: its roots striking in true humility deep into the grave of Jesus, the death to sin and self; its head lifted up in resurrection power to the heaven where Jesus is.

Believer, claim in faith the death and the life of Jesus as yours. Enter, in His grave, into the rest from self and its work—the rest of God. With Christ, who committed His spirit into the Father's hands, humble yourself and descend each day into that perfect, helpless dependence upon God. God will raise you up and exalt you.

Every morning, sink in deep, deep nothingness into the grave of Jesus. Every day, the life of Jesus will be manifest in you. Let a willing, loving, restful, happy humility be the mark that you have indeed claimed your birthright—the baptism into the death of Christ. "By one offering He hath perfected for ever them that are sanctified" (Hebrews 10:14). The souls that enter into His humiliation will find *in Him* the power to see and count self dead, and, as those who have learned and received of Him, to walk with all lowliness and meekness, supporting one another in love. The death-life is seen in a meekness and humility like that of Christ.

## Chapter 11

## HUMILITY AND HAPPINESS

*"Most gladly therefore will I rather glory in my infirmities, that the power of Christ may rest upon me. Therefore I take pleasure in infirmities: for when I am weak then am I strong"*—2 Corinthians 12:9-10.

In case Paul should exalt himself, by reason of the exceeding greatness of the revelations he had received from God, he was sent a thorn in the flesh to keep him humble. Paul's first desire was to have it removed, and three times he asked the Lord that it might depart. The answer came that the trial was a blessing; that, in the weakness and humiliation it brought, the grace and strength of the Lord could be better manifested. Paul at once entered into a new stage in his relationship to the trial. Instead of simply enduring it, *he most gladly gloried* in it. Instead of asking for deliverance, *he took pleasure* in it. He had learned that the place of humiliation is the place of blessing, of power, and of joy.

Virtually every Christian passes through these two stages in his pursuit of humility. In the first he fears and flees and seeks deliverance from all that can humble him. He has not yet learned to seek humility at any cost. He has accepted the command to be humble and seeks to obey it, though only to find out how utterly he fails. He prays for humility, at times very earnestly. But in his secret heart he prays more—if not in word, then in wish—to be kept from the very things that will make him humble. He is not yet so in love with humility as the beauty of the Lamb of God, and the joy of heaven, that he would sell all to procure it. In his pursuit of it, and his prayer for it, there is still somewhat of a sense of burden and of bondage. To humble himself has not yet become the spontaneous expression of a life and a nature that is essentially humble. It has not yet become his joy and only pleasure. He cannot yet say, "Most gladly do I glory in weakness; I take pleasure in whatever humbles me."

But can we hope to reach the stage in which this will be the case? Undoubtedly. And what will it be that brings us there? *That* which brought Paul there—*a new revelation of the Lord Jesus*. Nothing but the presence of God can reveal and expel self. A clearer insight was given to Paul into the deep truth that the presence of Jesus will banish every desire to seek anything in ourselves and will make us delight in every humiliation that prepares us for His fuller manifestation. Our humiliations lead us, in the experience of the presence and power of Jesus, to choose humility as our highest blessing. Let us try to learn the lessons the story of Paul teaches us.

We may have advanced believers, eminent teachers, and men of heavenly experiences, who have not yet fully learned the lesson of perfect humility, gladly glorying in weakness. We see this in Paul. The danger of exalting himself was coming very near. He did not yet know perfectly what it was to be nothing; to die, that Christ alone might live in him; to take pleasure in all that brought him low. It appears as if this were the highest lesson that he had to learn—full conformity to his Lord in that self-emptying where he gloried in weakness so that God might be all.

The highest lesson a believer has to learn is humility. Oh, that every Christian who seeks to advance in holiness may remember this well! There may be intense consecration and fervent zeal and heavenly experience, and yet, if it is not prevented by very special dealings of the Lord, there may be an unconscious self-exaltation with it all. Let us learn the lesson—the highest holiness is the deepest humility. Let us remember that it does not come by itself, but only as it is made a matter of special dealing on the part of our faithful Lord and His faithful servant.

Let us look at our lives in the light of this experience and see whether we gladly glory in weakness, whether we take pleasure, as Paul did, in trials, in necessities, and in distresses. Yes, let us ask whether we have learned to regard a reproof, just or unjust, a reproach from friend or enemy, trouble or difficulty into which others bring us, as, above all, an opportunity of proving how Jesus is all to us. It is an opportunity to prove how our own pleasure or honor are nothing, and how humiliation is, in very truth, what we take pleasure in. It is indeed blessed— the deep happiness of heaven—to be so free from self that whatever is said about us or done to us is lost and swallowed up in the thought that Jesus is all.

Let us trust Him who took charge of Paul to take charge of us, too. Paul needed special discipline, and special instruction, to learn what was more precious than even the unutterable things he had heard in heaven—what it is to glory in weakness and lowliness. We need it, too, oh so much. He who cared for Paul will care for us, too. He watches over us with a jealous, loving care, "lest we exalt ourselves." When we are doing so, He seeks to disclose to us the evil, and deliver us from it. In trial and weakness and trouble, He seeks to bring us low, until we learn that His grace is all, and to take pleasure in the very thing that brings us and keeps us low. His strength made perfect in our weakness, His presence filling and satisfying our emptiness, becomes the secret of a humility that need never fail. It can, as Paul, in full sight of what God works in and through us, always say, "In nothing was I behind the chiefest apostles, *though I am nothing"* (2 Corinthians 12:11). His humiliations had led him to true humility, with its wonderful gladness and glorying and pleasure in all that humbles.

"Most gladly will I rather glory in my infirmities, that the power of Christ may rest upon me; therefore I take pleasure in infirmities." The humble man has learned the secret of abiding gladness. The weaker he feels, the lower he sinks, and the greater his humiliations appear, the more the power and the presence of Christ are his portion. Then, as he says, "I am nothing," the Word of his Lord brings ever deeper joy: "My grace is sufficient for thee" (2 Corinthians 12:9).

I feel as if I must once again sum up all in these two lessons—the danger of pride is greater and nearer than we think, and the grace for humility is also.

*The danger of pride is greater and nearer than*

*we think*, especially at the time of our richest experiences. The preacher of spiritual truth with an admiring congregation hanging on his lips, the gifted speaker on a holiness platform expounding the secrets of the heavenly life, the Christian giving testimony to a blessed experience, the evangelist moving on in triumph and made a blessing to rejoicing multitudes—no man knows the hidden, the unconscious danger to which these are exposed. Paul was in danger without knowing it. What Jesus did for him is written for our admonition so that we may know our danger and know our only safety. Let it be said no more that a teacher or professor of holiness is full of self, or that he does not practice what he preaches, or that his blessing has not made him more humble or gentle. Jesus, in whom we trust, can make us humble.

*Yes, the grace for humility is greater and nearer, too, than we think.* The humility of Jesus is our salvation. Jesus Himself is our humility. Our humility is His care and His work. His grace is sufficient for us to meet the temptation of pride, too. His strength will be perfected in our weakness. Let us choose to be weak, to be low, to be nothing. Let humility be joy and gladness to us.

Let us gladly glory and take pleasure in weakness—in all that can humble us and keep us low. The power of Christ will rest upon us. Christ humbled Himself, therefore God exalted Him. Christ will humble us, and keep us humble. Let us heartily consent; let us trustfully and joyfully accept all that humbles. The power of Christ will rest upon us. We will find that the deepest humility is the secret of the truest happiness, of a joy that nothing can destroy.

## Chapter 12

## HUMILITY AND EXALTATION

*"He that humbleth himself shall be exalted"*—Luke 14:11; 18:14.

*"Humble yourself in the sight of the Lord, and He shall lift you up"*—James 4:10.

*"Humble yourselves therefore under the mighty hand of God, that He may exalt you in due time"*—1 Peter 5:6.

Just yesterday I was asked the question, How am I to conquer this pride? The answer was simple. Two things are needed. Do what God says is your work—humble yourself. Trust Him to do what He says is His work; He will exalt you.

The command is clear: humble yourself. That does not mean that it is your work to conquer and cast out the pride of your nature and to form within yourself the lowliness of the holy Jesus. No, this is God's work, the very essence of that exaltation in which He lifts you up into the real likeness of the beloved Son. What the command does mean is this—take every opportunity of humbling yourself before God and man. Humble yourself and stand persistently, not withstanding all failure and falling, under this unchanging command. Do this with faith in the grace that is already working in you and in the assurance that more grace will be available for the victory that is coming. Look to the light that conscience flashes on the pride of the heart and its workings.

Accept with gratitude everything that God allows from within or without, from friend or enemy, in nature or in grace, to remind you of your need of humbling, and to help you to it. Believe humility to indeed be the mother-virtue, your very first duty before God, and the one perpetual safeguard of the soul. Set your heart upon it as the source of all blessing. The promise is divine and sure, "He that humbleth himself shall be exalted." See that you do the one thing God asks: humble yourself. God will see that He does the one thing He has promised. He will give more grace; He will exalt you in due time.

All God's dealings with man are characterized by two stages. There is the time of preparation, when command and promise—with the mingled experience of effort and inability, of failure and partial success, with the holy expectancy of something better which these awaken—train and discipline men for a higher stage. Then comes the time of fulfillment, when faith inherits the promise and enjoys what it had so often struggled for in vain. This law holds good in every part of the Christian life and in the pursuit of every separate virtue. That is because it is grounded in the very nature of things.

In all that concerns our redemption, God must take the initiative. When that has been done, man's turn comes. In the effort after obedience and attainment, he must learn to know his weakness. In self-despair, he must learn to die to himself, and so be voluntarily and intelligently fitted to receive the promise from God. The Father will complete that which man had accepted at the beginning in ignorance. So God, who had been the beginning before man rightly knew Him or fully understood what His purpose was, is longed for and welcomed as the end—as the all in all.

It is even thus, too, in the pursuit of humility. To every Christian the command comes from the throne of God Himself: humble yourself. The earnest attempt to listen and obey will be rewarded—yes, rewarded—with the painful discovery of two things. The one, what depth of pride—unwillingness to count oneself and to be counted nothing, to submit absolutely to God—there was, that one never knew. The other, what utter weakness there is in all our efforts, and also in all our prayers for God's help, to destroy the hideous monster. Blessed is the man who now learns to put his hope in God and to persevere, notwithstanding all the power of pride within him, in acts of humility before God and men.

We know the law of human nature: acts produce habits; habits breed dispositions; dispositions form the will; and the rightly-formed will is character. It is not otherwise in the work of grace. As acts, persistently repeated, beget habits and dispositions, and these strengthen the will, He who works both to will and to do comes with His mighty power and Spirit. The humbling of the proud heart, with which the penitent saint casts himself so often before God, is rewarded with the "more grace" of the humble heart, in which the Spirit of Jesus has conquered and brought the new nature to its maturity. In this heart, He, the meek and lowly One, now dwells forever.

Humble yourselves in the sight of the Lord, and He will exalt you. And of what does the exaltation consist? The highest glory of man is in being only a vessel, to receive and enjoy and show forth the glory of God. It can do this only as it is willing to be nothing in itself so that God may be all. Water always fills the lowest places first. The lower, the emptier a man lies before God, the speedier and the fuller the inflow of the divine glory will be.

The exaltation God promises is not, cannot be, any external thing apart from Himself. All that He has to give or can give is only more of Himself, to take more complete possession. The exaltation is not, like an earthly prize, something arbitrary, in no necessary connection with the conduct to be rewarded. No, but it is in its very nature the effect and result of the humbling of ourselves. It is nothing but the gift of a divine indwelling humility—a conformity to and possession of the humility of the Lamb of God—which fits us for fully receiving the indwelling of God.

"He that humbleth himself shall be exalted." Jesus Himself is the proof of the truth of these words. He is the pledge of the certainty of their fulfillment to us. Let us take His yoke upon us and learn from Him, for He is meek and lowly of heart. If we are but willing to stoop to Him, as He has stooped to us, He will yet stoop to each one of us again, and we will find ourselves equally yoked with Him. As we enter deeper into the fellowship of His humility, and either humble ourselves or bear the humbling of men, we can count on the Spirit of His exaltation, "the Spirit of God and of glory," to rest upon us. The presence and the power of the glorified Christ will come to them who are of a humble spirit.

When God can again have His rightful place in us, He will lift us up. Make His glory your care in humbling yourself. He will make your glory His care in perfecting your humility, and breathing into you, as your abiding life, the very Spirit of His Son. As the all-pervading life of God possesses you, there will be nothing so natural and nothing so sweet as to be nothing, with not a thought or wish for self, because all is occupied with Him who fills all. "Most gladly therefore will I glory in my infirmities, that the power of Christ may rest upon me" (2 Corinthians 12:9).

Brethren, have we not here the reason that our consecration and our faith have availed so little in the pursuit of holiness? It was by self and its strength that the work was done under the name of faith. It was for self and its happiness that God was called in. It was, unconsciously, but still truly, in self and its holiness that the soul rejoiced. We never knew that humility— absolute, abiding, Christ-like humility, pervading and marking our whole life with God and man—was the most essential element of the life of the holiness we sought.

It is only in the possession of God that I lose myself. As it is in the height and breadth and glory of the sunshine that the littleness of a spec of dust playing in the sunlight is seen, so humility is our being, in God's presence, nothing but a speck dwelling in the sunlight of His love.

> "How great is God! how small am I!
> Lost, swallowed up in Love's immensity!
> God only there, not I."

May God teach us to believe that to be humble, to be nothing in His presence, is the highest attainment and the fullest blessing of the Christian life. He speaks to us: "I dwell in the high and holy place, and with him that is of a contrite and humble spirit" (Isaiah 57:15). Be this our destiny!

> "Oh, to be emptier, lowlier,
> Mean, unnoticed, and unknown,
> And to God a vessel holier,
> Filled with Christ, and Christ alone!"

# NOTES

Note A.—All this is to make it known that *pride* can degrade the highest angels into devils, and humility can raise fallen flesh and blood to the thrones of angels. Thus, this is the great end of God raising a new creation out of a fallen kingdom of angels. For this reason, it stands in its state of war between the fire and pride of fallen angels, and the humility of the Lamb of God. It is here that the last trumpet may sound the great truth through the depths of eternity: that evil can have no beginning but from pride, and no end but from humility.

The truth is this—pride must die in you, or nothing of heaven can live in you. Under the banner of the truth, give yourself up to the meek and humble spirit of the holy Jesus. Humility must sow the seed, or there can be no reaping in heaven. Do not look at pride as only an unbecoming temper, nor at humility as only a decent virtue. The one is death, and the other is life; the one is all hell, the other is all heaven.

As much as you have of pride within you, so you have of the fallen angel alive in you. As much as you have of true humility, so you have of the Lamb of God within you. If you could see what every stirring of pride does to your soul, you would beg of everything you meet to tear the viper from you, though with the loss of a hand or an eye. If you could see what a sweet, divine, transforming power there is in humility, how it expels the poison of your nature, and makes room for the Spirit of God to live in you, you would rather wish to be the footstool of all the world than lack the smallest degree of it.

Note B.—"We need to know two things: 1) That our salvation consists wholly in being saved from *ourselves*, or that which we are by nature; 2) That in the whole nature of things nothing could be this salvation or savior to us but such a humility of God as is beyond all expression. Hence the first unalterable term of the Savior to fallen man: Except a man denies *himself*, he cannot be My disciple (Matthew 16:24). Self is the whole evil of fallen nature; self-denial is our capacity of being saved. Humility is our savior. *Self* is the root, the branches, the tree, of all the evil of our fallen state. All the evils of fallen angels and men have their birth in the pride of self. On the other hand, all the virtues of the heavenly life are the virtues of humility. It is humility alone that makes the unpassable gulf between heaven and hell. What is then, or in what lies, the great struggle for eternal life? It lies entirely in the strife between *pride* and *humility*. Pride and humility are the two master powers—the two kingdoms in strife for the eternal possession of man.

"There never was, nor ever will be, but one humility, and that is the one humility of Christ. Pride and self have the all of man, until man has his all from Christ. He therefore only fights the good fight whose strife is that the self-idolatrous nature which he has from Adam may be brought to death by the supernatural humility of Christ brought to life in him."—William Law.

Note C.—"To die to self or come from under its power is not, cannot be, done by any active resistance we can make to it by the powers of nature. The one true way of dying to self is the way of *patience, meekness, humility, and resignation to God.* This is the truth and perfection of dying to self. For if I ask you what the Lamb of God means, must you not tell me that it is and means the perfection of *patience, meekness, humility, and resignation to God?* Must you not therefore say that a desire and faith in these virtues is an application to Christ, is a giving up of yourself to Him and the perfection of faith in

Him? And then, because this inclination of your heart to sink down in *patience, meekness, humility, and resignation to God* is truly giving up all that you are and all that you have from fallen Adam, it is leaving all you have to follow Christ. It is your highest act of faith in Him. Christ is nowhere but in these virtues. When they are there, He is in His own Kingdom. Let this be the Christ you follow.

"The Spirit of divine love can have no birth in any fallen creature, until it wills and chooses to be dead to all self, in a *patient, humble resignation* to the power and mercy of God.

"I seek all my salvation through the merits and mediation of the *meek, humble, patient, suffering Lamb of God.* He alone has the power to bring forth the blessed birth of these heavenly virtues in my soul. There is no possibility of salvation but in and by the birth of the *meek, humble, patient, resigned Lamb of God* in our souls. When the Lamb of God has brought forth a real birth of His own *meekness, humility, and full resignation to God* in our souls, then it is the birthday of the Spirit of love in our souls. Whenever we attain this, our souls will feast with such peace and joy in God as will blot out the remembrance of everything that we called peace or joy before.

"This way to God is infallible. This infallibility is grounded in the twofold character of our

Savior: 1) As He is the Lamb of God, a principle of all *meekness and humility* in the soul; 2) As He is the Light of heaven, and blesses eternal nature, and turns it into a Kingdom of heaven. When we are willing to get rest to our souls in *meek, humble resignation to God*, then it is that He, as the light of God and heaven, joyfully breaks in upon us. He turns our darkness into light and begins that Kingdom of God and of love within us, which will never have an end."— William Law.

Note D.—*A Secret of Secrets: Humility the Soul of True Prayer*. Until the spirit of the heart is renewed, until it is emptied of all earthly desires and stands in an habitual hunger and thirst after God—which is the true spirit of prayer—all our prayer will be too much like lessons given to scholars. We will mostly say them only because we dare not neglect them. But do not be discouraged. Take the following advice, and then you may go to church without any danger of mere lip service or hypocrisy, even though there is a hymn or a prayer whose language is higher than that of your heart. Do this: go to the church as the publican went to the temple. Stand inwardly in the spirit of your mind in that form which he outwardly expressed when he cast down his eyes and could only say, "God be merciful to me, a sinner" (Luke 18:13). Stand unchangeably, at least in your desire, in this form or state of heart. It will sanctify every petition that comes out of your mouth. When anything is read or sung or prayed that is more exalted than your heart is, make this an occasion of further sinking down in the spirit of the publican. You will then be helped and highly blessed by those prayers and praises which seem only to belong to a heart better than yours.

This, my friend, is a secret of secrets. It will help you to reap where you have not sown, and it will be a continual source of grace in your soul. For everything that inwardly stirs in you, or outwardly happens to you, becomes a real good to you if it finds or excites in you *this humble state of mind.* For nothing is in vain, or without profit to *the humble soul.* It stands always in a state of divine growth; everything that falls upon it is like a dew of heaven to it. Shut yourself up, therefore, in this *form of humility.* All good is enclosed in it; it is a water of heaven that turns the fire of the fallen soul into the meekness of the divine life and creates that oil out of which the love to God and man gets its flame. Always be enclosed in it—let it be as a garment wherewith you are always covered, and as a girdle with which you are girt. Breathe nothing but in and from its spirit. See nothing but with its eyes. Hear nothing but with its ears. And then, whether you are in the church or out of the church, hearing the praises of God or receiving wrongs from men and the world, all will be edification, and everything will help your growth in the life of God move forward.

## A PRAYER FOR HUMILITY

Here I will give you an infallible touchstone that will tie all to the truth. It is this; retire from the world and all conversation, only for one month. Neither write, nor read, nor debate anything with yourself. Stop all the former workings of your heart and mind. And, with all the strength of your heart, stand all this month, as continually as you can, in the following form of prayer to God. Offer it frequently on your knees. But whether sitting, walking, or standing, be always inwardly longing and earnestly praying this one prayer to God:

"That of His great goodness He would make known to you, and take from your heart, *every kind and form and degree of pride*, whether it be from evil spirits, or your own corrupt nature; and that He would awaken in you the *deepest depth and truth of that humility* which can make you capable of His light and Holy Spirit."

Reject every thought, but that of waiting and

praying in this matter from the bottom of your heart, with such truth and earnestness, as people in torment wish to pray and be delivered from it. If you can and will give yourself up in truth and sincerity to this spirit of prayer, I will venture to affirm that, if you had twice as many evil spirits in you as Mary Magdalene had, they will all be cast out of you, and you will be forced with her to weep tears of love at the feet of the holy Jesus.

# ANOTHER POWERFUL Book

## from Whitaker House

**Divine Healing**

*Andrew Murray*

Why are some people healed while others are not? What part do doctors play in divine healing? Is it God's will to heal the sick? Does sickness come from God or from Satan? There are many questions about divine healing. Writing from his own experience, Murray examines what the Bible says about sickness and what we can do to obtain healing in Christ.

ISBN: 0-88368-642-2 • Trade • 160 pages